TAKE TEN YEARS

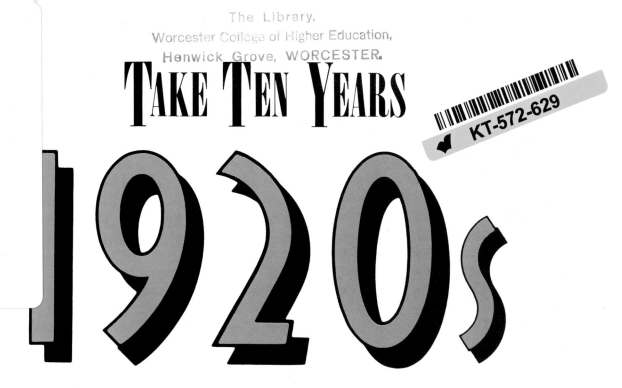

1920s

Books are
the

MARGARET SHARMAN

EVANS BROTHERS LIMITED

Contents

The pictures on page 4 show
A bomb explodes in Dublin, Ireland during the civil war
Starving Russian peasants leaving their lands
State troopers unloading captured alcohol during America's prohibition era
Recording a radio programme

The pictures on page 5 show
Sailors unloading rations at a London power station, protected by soldiers, in the General Strike
Josef Stalin
General strike, improvised transport in London streets
Houdini poster

Introduction

After World War I (then called the Great War), European countries had to rebuild everything: their homes, their industries and even their lives. Men returning from the war found no work. First the factories and the shops had to be rebuilt, and markets found for their products.

Almost every European country was affected. Before the war, Turkey and Austria had large empires. Both fought on the losing side, and after the war the countries they had occupied became new small nations. These nations had to learn to manage their own affairs. In Germany and Italy, the standard of living was very low after the war. New political parties, the Nazis and the Fascists, took over the weak governments there.

Women had the vote, and some had jobs. Their clothing showed that they no longer stayed at home all day – skirts were shorter and more practical for walking in the streets or catching a bus. The huge hats they used to wear were gone, and would never come back.

To forget the gloom of the war years young people went to 'tea dances', where they danced the Charleston. It was fashionable to smoke cigarettes, through long thin cigarette-holders, and drink cocktails. They listened to jazz. The lucky ones owned a wireless set.

In America, alcohol was banned, but it was not difficult to get 'bootleg' gin (so called because in the old days smugglers hid bottles in their sea-boots, and were known as 'bootleggers'). The country was very prosperous, and Americans were loving their new wealth. They bought huge houses. They gave parties. They drove Model T Fords or Chevrolets. They swooned over Rudolf Valentino in *The Sheikh*. They invested their new wealth in stocks and shares, and the profits went up and up. Then, right at the end of the decade, the stock market collapsed. Shares were worth nothing. The unbelievable had happened; the Great Depression began on both sides of the Atlantic.

YEARS	WORLD AFFAIRS
1920	Turkey and Austria lose their Empires
1921	Germany: the Reparations Bill European unemployment Anglo-Irish Treaty
1922	Egypt becomes a Kingdom Italy has a Fascist government Turks threaten the Dardanelles
1923	Economic crisis in Germany Russia becomes the USSR French occupy the Ruhr
1924	Stalin takes over leadership of USSR
1925	Italy becomes a dictatorship Prosperity in USA
1926	General Strike in Britain Kingdom of Saudi Arabia recognized
1927	Nationalists challenge Communists in China
1928	Stalin in full control of USSR
1929	The Wall Street Crash Creation of Vatican City Mustafa Kemal's reforms in Turkey

WARS & CIVIL DISORDER	PEOPLE	EVENTS
Civil war in Ireland	Gandhi emerges as Indian nationalist Harding becomes US President	League of Nations begins work Prohibition of alcohol in USA Olympic Games in Antwerp
	Keynes predicts economic disaster Marie Stopes opens birth control clinic Banting and Best discover insulin	First 'Miss America' beauty competition
The IRA split into two parties and fight each other End of war between Turkey and Greece Civil disobedience in India	Michael Collins, head of Irish Free State, shot dead Victor Sylvester, ballroom dancing king Mussolini leads Italy's Fascists	New pope elected BBC formed Pharaoh Tutankhamun's tomb found
Ku Klux Klan active in southern states of USA	Röntgen, Nobel Prize winner, dies Duke of York marries Suzanne Lenglen wins at Wimbledon Coolidge becomes US President	British railways reorganized Earthquake in Japan Football crowd overflow Wembley Stadium
	Mallory and Irvine lost on Everest Schweitzer rebuilds hospital in West Africa Mateotti, Mussolini's critic, murdered Elgar, composer, honoured	Two general elections in UK British Empire Exhibition Olympic Games in Paris
	Carter reveals Tutankhamun's mummy Louis Armstrong promotes jazz Hitler publishes *Mein Kampf*	Britain returns to gold standard, fixing the value of the pound Darwin's evolution theory on trial in USA Chaplin film, *The Gold Rush*
	Birth of Princess Elizabeth Death of actor Rudolf Valentino Jack Hobbs has record batting score	Ancient skull found in South Africa Television demonstrated for the first time
Chiang Kai-shek opposes China's warlords	Sir Henry Wood conducts first broadcast Promenade Concert Baseball hero 'Babe' Ruth scores record runs Lindbergh flies Atlantic Menuhin plays violin in London	First talking picture, *The Jazz Singer*
Chinese and Japanese clash	Walt Disney creates Mickey Mouse Campbell breaks land speed record	British women over 21 given the vote Olympic Games in Amsterdam Mt. Etna erupts
	Fleming discovers penicillin Marx Brothers make a film Hitchcock produces first talking film	Gangsters shot in St. Valentine's Day massacre in USA Airship flies round the world

1920

A NEW INTERNATIONAL ORGANIZATION

Feb 11, London   Forty-two countries have become members of a new League of Nations. The Great War ended only 15 months ago, and the members hope to stop such wars in the future.

The League will ask the major powers to help support smaller or weaker countries. These countries will be called 'mandates'. Many of the countries that will become mandates were once part of the Turkish and Austrian Empires, which have now been broken up.

It is disappointing that America has so far declined to join the League.

TURKEY HAS LOST ITS EMPIRE

August 10, Sèvres, France   By a new treaty, Greece has won a large part of the old Turkish Empire. Hejaz in Arabia is now an independent country. Syria has already become a mandate of France; Mesopotamia and Palestine are new British mandates. The Dardanelles, where heavy fighting took place during the war, has been made an international zone. British, French and Italian troops are guarding it.

HUNGARY'S BORDERS SHRINK

June 4, Versailles, France   Hungary has been part of the Austrian Empire for 50 years. Now the northern area, where the Czechs and Slovaks live, will become Czechoslovakia. The southern part will be united with Yugoslavia. Hungary, with its capital at Budapest, is now less than a third of its size before the war.

A VOICE AGAINST THE EMPIRE

Sept 10, Delhi   Mr. Mohandas Gandhi, a young Indian lawyer who trained in Britain, wants the British to leave India. He suggests that Indians stop co-operating with them. They will not import British textiles, but will spin and weave their own cloth.

HUNGARY'S NEW BORDERS

ESTONIA
LATVIA
LITHUANIA
Danzig
POLAND
GERMANY
RUSSIA
CZECHOSLOVAKIA
SWITZ.   AUSTRIA   HUNGARY   TRANSYLVANIA   BESSARABIA
YUGOSLAVIA   ROMANIA
ITALY   Black Sea
BULGARIA
ALBANIA
GREECE   TURKEY

0   km   500

▨ Old Austro-Hungarian Empire
–·— Post 1920 boundaries

STRONG DRINK IS ILLEGAL

May 30, Chicago On January 16 it became illegal to buy or drink alcohol in any American state. Already 'prohibition' has led to a black market in alcohol. Crooks have quickly realized that they can make big money by importing it illegally. These 'bootleggers' give the police big bribes to 'look the other way'. Most citizens also turn a blind eye because they want to go on buying whisky and gin.

CIVIL WAR FLARES UP IN IRELAND

Dec 23, Ireland The Catholic nationalist party, Sinn Fein ('We ourselves'), wants Ireland to break away from the United Kingdom. Sinn Fein's fighting force, the Irish Republican Army (IRA), is attacking pro-British Irish people, and damaging government property. British ex-servicemen have been sent to Ireland to help the regular troops. They are known as the 'Black and Tans' because of the colour of their uniforms. They are becoming as violent as the IRA. There is now a civil war in Ireland.

Black and Tans search a Sinn Feiner.

AMERICA HAS A NEW PRESIDENT

Nov 2, Washington Mr. Warren Harding is the new President of the United States. This is the first election in which women were allowed to vote for a president. They fought for this right for nearly 50 years. Mr. Harding's campaign song, 'You're the man for us', was written by a young singer called Al Jolson.

UNKNOWN SOLDIERS REST IN PEACE

November 11, London The body of an unidentified soldier, who died fighting in France, has been brought to England by sea. He will be buried in Westminster Abbey. His grave is a symbol for all those who died in the Great War of 1914–18. In France, an unknown soldier has been buried in Paris, under the Arc de Triomphe.

The tomb of the Unknown Soldier in London

THE BOLSHEVIKS WIN RUSSIA'S CIVIL WAR

Nov 20, Petrograd The Bolsheviks (Communists) formed a government in Russia three years ago, but thousands of Russians have been fighting against them. Now, after a fierce battle, their White Army has been defeated by the Bolshevik Red Army. All Russians now have to accept Lenin's Communist government.

NEWS IN BRIEF . . .

HOUSING SHORTAGE

Jan 9, London First-time buyers of houses have had a difficult time lately. Hardly any houses have been built since 1914. Now the government has plans for 100,000 new homes. In addition, a new city is being built. It will be called Welwyn Garden City.

London slum dwellers now hope for new housing.

AIR TRANSPORT HAS ARRIVED!

July 5, London England's first airport has been built at Croydon. Not many people use air transport yet, but soon we may all 'take to the skies'. Today letters were carried by a new airmail service, to Amsterdam.

The controllers at Croydon keep track of aircraft on a large map in the control tower. A wireless operator keeps in touch with the pilots. The operator can plot on a map the position of an aeroplane within three kilometres (about 1½ miles).

AMERICANS EXCEL AT OLYMPIC GAMES

Sept 12, Antwerp, Belgium The seventh Olympic Games ended today in Belgium. This is the first time the games have been held since the war. In all, 29 nations took part. A 13-year-old American girl, Aileen Riggen, won the springboard diving competition. Her gold medal was one of 41 won by the United States – a remarkable achievement. The first ice hockey matches to be played at the Olympics were greatly enjoyed by spectators. The ice hockey was won by a team from Canada.

FASHIONS INFLUENCED BY THE WAR

Nov 11, London This is the second anniversary of the ending of the Great War. During the war, from 1914 to 1918, hundreds of women worked to help the war effort. They had to wear clothes that were shorter and more practical. Today's fashions for women are comfortable and casual. The waistline has dropped to the hip, and skirt hems fall just above the ankle. Fashionable ladies have had their long hair cut short, and waved.

Smart young women are having their hair 'bobbed'.

HUNDREDS HEAR FAMOUS SOPRANO

June 15, Chelmsford, England Dame Nellie Melba, the celebrated Australian singer, is the first person to broadcast a musical programme. Today she sang on the air from the Marconi Wireless Station. The broadcasting engineer showed her the wireless mast with its aerial. "Your voice will be sent all over England from there," he said. At first Dame Melba thought she had to climb the mast and sing through the aerial!

Some wireless owners are buying loudspeakers, but most people 'listen in' alone, with headphones.

HOW LONG DO WE LIVE?

Dec, Washington A recent survey published here shows that an average American man lives 53½ years. An American woman lives one year longer. Life expectancy has gone up remarkably in recent year. Twenty years ago a man might expect to live only until he was 49.

1921

UNEMPLOYMENT IS WORLD-WIDE
DOLE QUEUES ARE LONGER

Feb 16, London A million men are out of work in England. An unemployment benefit (the 'dole') pays 18 shillings a week (15 shillings for women). This is hardly enough even to feed a family, let alone buy clothes or shoes. Many children are going barefoot as parents simply cannot afford to replace outgrown shoes.

Many out-of-work men are selling matches or bootlaces in the streets. Others play musical instruments or sing, hoping that passers-by will give them a few coins. Ex-soldiers were told they were returning to 'a land fit for heroes'. Many feel more like outcasts. They see no hope of getting a job and a decent wage in post-war Britain.

Ex-soldiers hawk their wares.

GERMAN MARKS ARE ALMOST WORTHLESS

Nov 7, Germany Britain and France have sent Germany a bill for £10 billion. They need these 'reparations' to pay their own war debts, and to rebuild France and Belgium. The French have occupied the Ruhr, Germany's industrial centre. They will take coal away as their share of the reparations. Germany's financial crisis has made its currency very weak. Seven years ago one English pound was worth 20 marks. Today you would need 1200 marks in exchange for a pound. The government has resigned. A small political party, the National Socialists (Nazis), blames Jews and capitalists. The leader of the party is Herr Adolf Hitler.

German children play with bundles of banknotes. German currency is virtually waste paper.

Coal strikers rally to hear a speaker in Wigan.

THE MINERS ARE ON STRIKE

April 15, northern England British coalminers have been striking for two weeks now. Many miners had good wages during the war because coal sold well. There was no competition from cheap coal from abroad. Now the price of coal has fallen. Wages are going down, and the miners will have to work longer hours. Because of the strike, miners' wives and children are short of food and fuel.

RUSSIANS ARE DYING OF HUNGER

Aug 4, St. Petersburg There is mass unemployment in Russia. The civil war interfered with farming and the economy suffered. The harvest failed, following a long drought. Many villages are reporting epidemics of the diseases cholera and typhoid. Up to 20,000 people face starvation. Lenin has asked other countries for help for the starving.

Russian children are suffering from famine.

THE LEAGUE OF NATIONS SOLVES TWO DISPUTES

Sept 22, Geneva Three Balkan countries, Latvia, Lithuania and Estonia, have joined the League of Nations. The League of Nations has already settled two international problems. Last year Sweden and Finland disagreed about possession of a small island. This year the League settled a frontier dispute between Turkey and Iraq (formerly Mesopotamia). These were minor problems, but the results are encouraging for the League's future.

Michael Collins, head of the Irish Free State

American Businesses Face a Recession

Sept 26, New York Nearly four million people are unemployed in America. The government is going to create jobs for as many as possible. Immigration has been restricted. The country cannot afford to take in any more unemployed foreigners.

REPARATIONS ARE WRONG, SAYS EXPERT

Dec, Cambridge, England A British economist, Mr. John Maynard Keynes, has said that the former Allies are wrong to make Germany pay the huge reparations bill. It is too much for any country to pay. No country stands alone, he says. Germany's bankruptcy may have a knock-on effect all over Europe. This in turn could easily lead to hardship, revolts and uprisings. The peace Europe needs so badly seems hard to find.

NAVAL TREATY ENDS WARSHIP BUILDING

Dec 14, Washington By a treaty signed yesterday, the United States, Britain, France and Japan agreed to limit the number of warships each may have. This means that Britain will no longer have the largest fleet of ships in the world. Over 650 British ships will have to be scrapped. Many dockers and shipbuilders will lose their jobs.

IRELAND IS DIVIDED

Dec 6, Downing Street, London Today British ministers signed a treaty with members of Sinn Fein which made southern Ireland independent of the United Kingdom. There are 32 counties in Ireland; 26 have joined together as the Irish Free State. The other six, to be called Northern Ireland, will remain part of the United Kingdom. The British government hopes that this will end the bitter fighting in Ireland. But Mr. Michael Collins, who signed the treaty for Ireland, knows that many southerners want the whole of Ireland to be independent. "I have signed my death warrant," he said. Nobody knows how seriously he meant this. He certainly has many enemies.

NEWS IN BRIEF . . .

DR. STOPES BACKS BIRTH CONTROL

Mar 18, London Over a shop door in a London street is a notice saying 'Mothers' Clinic for Constructive Birth Control'. The clinic is run by Dr. Marie Stopes. She believes that married women should decide how many children they have. But many doctors and clergymen say birth control is immoral. Women will have to make up their own minds on this issue.

DIABETES SUFFERERS CAN HOPE FOR RELIEF

July 30, Toronto, Canada Dr. Frederick Banting and Dr. Charles Best have discovered that people who have diabetes can be helped by injections of insulin. When this treatment is available, sufferers may hope to live longer. At present, if you are diagnosed as diabetic, you will probably live for less than five years.

Dr. Marie Stopes.

CARUSO IS DEAD

Aug 3, New York Enrico Caruso, the leading Italian tenor, has died at the age of 48. He was born in Naples. In his twenties he sang in operas at the famous La Scala Opera House in Milan. For the last 18 years he has been the principal tenor at New York's Metropolitan Opera House. Thousands of copies of his gramophone records have been sold all over the world. They have brought him a great deal of fame – and money.

LITTLE MISS AMERICA IS CROWNED

Sept 7, Atlantic City A blonde, blue-eyed girl of 16 has become the first 'Miss America'. Eight girls entered the contest. Already dozens are preparing for the next one. The city's businessmen believe a yearly competition will be good for the tourist trade.

Miss Margaret Gorman, the first Miss America

PRINCE IS LEADER OF FASHION

Nov 17, London The Prince of Wales has landed in Bombay for a long tour of India. His clothes are influencing men's wear. The Prince wears narrow lapels and padded shoulders. Shoes, rather than boots, are now worn. Trilby hats have wide brims and broad ribbons, sometimes coming halfway up the crown. For many men, a pipe and a stick are essential accessories.

Wristwatches are taking the place of the large pocket watch, with its safety-chain attached to a buttonhole in the waistcoat. These extra buttonholes are disappearing.

The Prince of Wales (second from right) as leader of fashion

1922

IRELAND

SOUTHERNERS DISAGREE WITH ANGLO-IRISH TREATY

May 31, Dublin   Mr. Michael Collins, head of the Irish Free State government, has a grave problem. The 'republicans', those who do not want a separate Irish Free State, are in revolt. They have murdered soldiers, and in April seized the Court House. Some of the republicans were Mr. Collins's most trusted men. Many Irishmen who served in the British Army have joined the army of the Free State. The republicans say this is the same army with a new name. They are bitter because Mr. Collins is using the army against them. They think he has betrayed southern Ireland.

COLLINS SENDS IN THE TROOPS

Aug 15, Dublin   In June Mr. Collins sent Free State troops to force the republicans out of Dublin's Court House. He also sent troops to besiege republicans in Cork. He is now the most hated man in the Irish government.

COLLINS GUNNED DOWN IN CORK

Aug 22, Cork   Mr. Collins has been shot dead in an ambush. He came to Cork, where he was born, two days ago. He said to friends, "They won't shoot me in my own country". He was 31 years old. The army of the Free State has been told not to avenge his death.

Riflemen of the Irish Free State. Using a hole already made by gunfire, they are sniping at the Dublin rebels.

THE FREE STATE STANDS ALONE

Dec 17, Dublin   British troops have left the IFS, which now has no official ties with Britain.

A NEW GOVERNMENT IN ITALY

THE FASCIST LEADER PERMITS ILLEGAL ACTS

Jan 30, Milan Italy's government is weak and its economy poor. The Communists want a Russian-type government. Others are joining Signor Benito Mussolini's Fascists in Milan. The Fascists are known to physically attack Communists, many of whom have been 'beaten up'. There are 35 Fascists in Italy's parliament, the Chamber of Deputies.

'BLACKSHIRTS' SEIZE POWER

Aug 3, Milan Dressed in their uniform of brown trousers and black shirts, the Fascists under Benito Mussolini marched into Milan's industrial area and stopped a general strike. They terrorized the workers and burnt trade union buildings. Police and troops were unable to stop them.

FASCIST LEADER IS NEW PRIME MINISTER

Nov 25, Rome Last month 24,000 Fascists marched into Rome from Milan. The King of Italy was afraid of their strength. He asked Signor Mussolini to lead the government. Signor Mussolini has now become the dictator of Italy. He has told the Chamber of Deputies that all members must obey him. They have meekly agreed.

Mussolini (second from right) with fellow Fascists.

INDIAN NATIONALIST JAILED

March 18, Ahmedabad, Gujarat Mr. Gandhi's policy of non-cooperation with the British has led to civil disobedience. People are refusing to pay their taxes. A British magistrate sentenced Mr. Gandhi to six years' imprisonment for encouraging people to break the law. The magistrate said he realized that to millions of people Mr. Gandhi was "a great patriot and a great leader".

THE NEW POPE APPEALS FOR PEACE

Feb 6, Rome Cardinal Achille Ratti has been elected pope, just three weeks after the previous pope died. He has chosen the name Pius XI. After the election the Pope went out onto the balcony of St. Peter's and blessed the crowd. He prayed for "that peace for which the world sighs so much".

PHARAOH'S TOMB IS OPENED

Nov 30, Thebes, Egypt There was great excitement yesterday in a desert valley here. Dr. Howard Carter has discovered the tomb of Pharoah Tutankhamun, who lived 3000 years ago. Dr. Carter tells us what happened as he opened the tomb:

"At first I could see nothing, the hot air escaping from the chamber causing the candle to flicker. But presently, as my eyes grew accustomed to the light, details of the room emerged slowly from the mist, strange animals, statues, and gold – everywhere the glint of gold. For a moment – an eternity it must have seemed to the others standing by, I was struck dumb; then Lord Carnarvon inquired anxiously – 'Can you see anything?'"

'Yes,' I replied, . . . 'wonderful things. . .' "

EGYPT HAS A KING

March 16, Cairo The people of Egypt are jubilant because the British protectorate over Egypt has ended after 40 years. The Sultan of Egypt has become King Fuad I. Coins will be struck in his name, and stamps will bear his portrait.

KEMAL'S VICTORY THREATENS STRAITS

Oct 30, Turkey Since 1920, when the Greeks were given much of Turkey's territory, the Turkish army has been fighting to regain the land. This army, led by Mustafa Kemal, has reached the Dardanelles. The Turks want to control these important straits, which are a neutral zone.

(*The Tomb of Tutankhamun*, Vol. 1, Howard Carter and A.C. Mace, Cassell plc, 1923)

NEWS IN BRIEF . . .

THE MEDIEVAL LOOK IS MODERN

April 30, London This year, evening clothes have low waistlines, wide sleeves and trailing hems. Long bead necklaces complete the ensemble. The fashion designers say they are influenced by medieval clothing. What is not medieval is the new bust bodice. It flattens the bosom to give a boyish line. The flatter you are, the better!

'Flappers' – the new slang word for fashionable young women – wear their hair bobbed, with a bandeau over the forehead.

TRAVEL MADE EASY

Sept 4, London A new factory is producing sidecars for motor cycles. They will be popular with young couples, though they give the passenger a bumpy ride. The new Morris Oxford cars, and the Austin Sevens (Baby Austins) are both on sale now. They are quite easy to drive when you have mastered the 'double declutching' as you change gear. And you don't need to pass any test to drive on British roads. The speed limit is 20 mph.

LONDONER WINS CHAMPIONSHIP

Dec, London Mr. Victor Sylvester has won the World Professional Ballroom Dancing Championship, partnered by his wife. Victor is the son of a London clergyman. Besides the foxtrot, slow foxtrot and waltz, Victor is proficient in the more exotic tango and rumba.

The cast of the first BBC wireless revue programme

Mr. and Mrs. Victor Sylvester

HEAR THE NEWS ON THE DAY IT HAPPENS

Nov 15, London Today a news bulletin was read over the air for the first time, from the newly-formed British Broadcasting Corporation (BBC). Although you cannot see them, radio announcers and performers wear evening dress when they are broadcasting.

ULYSSES IS BANNED AND BURNT

March 5, New York On Mr. James Joyce's fortieth birthday, February 2, his new novel, *Ulysses*, was published in Paris. Today a newspaper reviewer called it a work of genius, but did not like its vulgarity. Mr. Joyce uses some words which are not generally seen in print. The book is banned in Britain and America. When someone tried to mail copies to New York, the Post Office seized and burnt them. Some British travellers have succeeded in smuggling copies past the Customs officers.

1923

CHAOS IN GERMANY

WORKERS ARE RIOTING IN THE RUHR

Jan 25, Weimar There was trouble in the Ruhr this month. The German chancellor told factory workers and miners to work to rule. But many refused to work at all, and went on strike. They abused French troops as they loaded coal onto trucks to take to France. Fighting broke out, and the French arrested many of the workers.

THE FRENCH MAKE THE CRISIS WORSE

Feb 1, Weimar The French are preventing coal from reaching German factories and homes. There is less and less to buy in the shops. Food is very expensive. The value of one pound is now 220,000 marks. The Bavarians of south-east Germany have set up a dictatorship of their own. They have no faith in the German government.

CARTER IN TUTANKHAMUN'S CHAMBER

Feb 20, Cairo It has taken Dr. Howard Carter many months to clear the first room of Tutankhamun's tomb. Three days ago he carefully removed the wall that seals the burial chamber. There he found, and opened, an enormous gold shrine. Inside there were three more shrines, each smaller than the last. The fourth contained a stone coffin decorated at each corner with a winged goddess. It may contain the Pharaoh's body.

DUKE OF YORK MARRIES

April 26, London The Duke of York married Lady Elizabeth Bowes-Lyon in Westminster Abbey today. The Church of England would not allow the service to be broadcast, in case people in public houses listened to the service with disrespect. The Duke is second in line to the throne, after his brother, the Prince of Wales.

The royal bride leaves home for the Abbey.

DISCOVERER OF X-RAYS DIES

Feb 10, Germany Dr. Wilhelm Röntgen, who won the Nobel Prize in 1901 for discovering X-rays, died yesterday. X-rays are used to show the bones and internal organs of the body. They help doctors to diagnose disease, and surgeons to perform operations. Röntgen refused to make any money from his discovery, and he died penniless.

THERE ARE NOW FOUR RAILWAY COMPANIES

Jan 1, London   The 120 railway companies of Great Britain have been reorganized into four groups: the Great Western Railway (GWR), the London, Midland & Scottish (LMS), the London & North Eastern (LNER), and the Southern Railway (SR). Although some suburban trains now run on electricity, the main trains will run on steam power for some time to come.

RUSSIA HAS A NEW NAME

July 6, Moscow   Russia is to be called the Union of Soviet Socialist Republics (USSR). The country is a collection of different republican councils ('soviets') under one central government. It contains about 100 different nationalities. Lenin, the Bolshevik leader, is trying to mould them all into one nation, led by the Communist Party.

ILLEGAL SOCIETY USES VIOLENCE

Sept 15, Oklahoma   A society known as the Ku Klux Klan (KKK) is causing racial hatred in America. Klan members dress in white robes. Pointed hoods leave only their eyes showing. They terrorize Indians, Negroes, Jews and Catholics, whom they call 'un-American'. Oklahoma's governor has formed a national guard to stop this violent behaviour, but in other southern states the KKK continue their terrorism unchecked.

Klansmen may look absurd, but they are killers.

TERRIBLE EARTHQUAKE IN JAPAN

Sept 3, Tokyo   News is coming through of a severe earthquake in Tokyo. It happened two days ago, when workers were going home to lunch. In some areas the ground rose up by three metres (nine feet). Japanese houses are made of wood and paper. Many caught fire when the earthquake overturned lamps and cooking stoves. Other fires were started by broken electric cables and gas mains. Altogether about 100,000 people have died, and 2½ million are homeless. Half the city is completely destroyed.

The Japanese city of Yokohama devastated by the earthquake. A terrible fire followed.

PRESIDENT DIES, VICE-PRESIDENT SWORN IN

Aug 3, Washington   Mr. Calvin Coolidge, the Vice-President, was today sworn in as the new President of the United States. The former president, Mr. Warren Harding, died of a stroke on his return home from a hectic business trip.

President Coolidge agrees with the US policy not to join the League of Nations. He has been elected as the economy is beginning to improve. Americans feel that better times are on the way.

THE TURKS WIN THE DARDANELLES

July 24, Turkey Mustafa Kemal and his Turkish army have won the battle for the Dardanelles. The British have agreed to leave the former neutral zone. A million Greeks are now living in Turkish territory. There are almost as many Turks in Greece. The League of Nations is going to try to exchange the two 'foreign' populations.

Mustafa Kemal (left), the victorious Turkish general

THE MARK TOPPLES STILL FURTHER

Sept 12, Weimar A pound is now equal to a staggering 600,000,000 marks. You need a suitcase full of money when you go shopping. Germany has a new chancellor, Dr. Gustav Stresemann. He has ordered strikers in the Ruhr to return to work. He believes that co-operation with the rest of Europe is a better policy than resistance.

At a rally in Nuremburg this week Herr Adolf Hitler strongly criticized the government.

A new German banknote for 20 million marks

BANKS WILL BUY YOUR MONEY

Nov 15, Weimar The government is asking people to return their paper money to the bank. In exchange, everyone will get new coins and notes. The Allies are going to reconsider the way in which reparations should be paid.

HITLER IS IN JAIL

Nov 12, Munich Four days ago Herr Hitler, with a group of Nazis, burst into a beer hall where a Bavarian official was making a speech. He fired a shot into the air. "The revolution has begun," he shouted. He then led the Nazis towards the town square, but they were stopped by police. Many were arrested. Herr Hitler is in jail. Another Nazi, Herr Hermann Goering, was badly wounded and is in hospital. The Bavarians refused to support this attempt at a national revolution.

NEWS IN BRIEF . . .

POLICEMAN SAVES CUP FINAL

April 28, London A policeman kept his head today and probably saved many lives. West Ham United was playing Bolton Wanderers in the final of the FA Cup. The new Wembley stadium is built for about 100,000 people, but twice that number were let into the ground. Thousands of spectators were pushed down onto the pitch.

Policeman George Storey, on a white horse, managed to keep order until police reinforcements arrived. Nobody was hurt. After a late start, a cheerful crowd watched the Wanderers win by two goals to one.

RIN TIN TIN IS FAMOUS

Dec, Hollywood During the Great War (1914-18), an American soldier found a starving German shepherd dog in the trenches in France. He adopted it, and brought it home. The dog, Rin Tin Tin, is now working in films. He is such a popular star that he has his own fan mail. His latest film is *The Night Cry*.

Rin Tin Tin goes to the rescue in *Tracked by the Police*.

LENGLEN WINS ONCE MORE

July 15, Wimbledon The heroine of women's tennis, Suzanne Lenglen, has won the women's singles for the third time. The French player was also in the winning women's doubles, and the mixed doubles. Miss Lenglen has amazing control and perfect footwork. She volleys much more often and with greater effect than other women players. She has won every tournament in France since 1920, and in that year took a gold medal at the Olympic Games.

DANCING FOR PROFIT IS NO FUN

April 14, New York The dance marathon is the new craze in America. The record for non-stop dancing is 90 hours. This strenuous exercise is a danger to health. Couples have been taken to hospital after collapsing on the dance floor. When he had danced for 86 hours one young man fell down dead. Why do they do it? There is a big cash prize for the record-breaker.

A girl collapses in exhaustion at a dance marathon in America.

1924

ATROCITY IN ITALY

FASCISTS WIN THE ELECTIONS

April 17, Rome The Fascists have won the general election by a huge majority. Signor Mussolini and his party are back in power. The Communist candidates were heavily defeated. Italians hope that the Fascists will bring in much-needed reforms.

MUSSOLINI'S CRITIC IS KIDNAPPED

June 10, Rome In May, Socialist landowner Giacomo Matteotti accused the Fascists of rigging the election. He said they used threats and cheated. He is an outspoken critic of the Fascists. Now Signor Matteotti has disappeared. Passers-by on a busy street in Rome watched horrified as he was bundled into a car. The car drove off at high speed. The Fascists are suspected of organizing the kidnapping.

MISSING LANDOWNER FOUND DEAD

Aug 17, Rome Signor Matteotti's body was found yesterday in a shallow grave a few miles from Rome. He had been beaten to death. The people of Rome have laid flowers on the pavement where he was kidnapped. His widow is sure that the Fascists are responsible. She has appealed to Signor Mussolini to return her husband's body, but the Fascist leader denies all knowledge of the killing. There are no clues as to who murdered him.

LABOUR IS IN

Jan 23, London The Labour party has won the general election. Mr. Ramsay MacDonald is the first Labour Prime Minister. For the first time Britain will have working-class men in the government and the Cabinet. They will try to ease unemployment, and revive British industry.

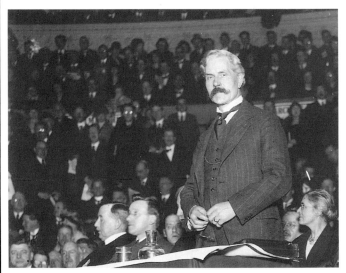

Mr. Ramsay MacDonald at the victory demonstration

NOVEL SHOWS INDIAN DILEMMA

Feb 4, London Mr. E. M. Forster's new novel *A Passage to India* is about relationships between Indians and the British. Empire-builders think there should be no social contact between the two. Mr. Forster shows the misery that such attitudes, and such relationships, bring. The book may make Europeans more sympathetic to Mr. Gandhi's views. The Indian leader was freed today after serving two years of his six-year sentence.

COMRADE LENIN DIES

Jan 21, Moscow Vladimir Lenin is dead. Seven years ago he led the successful revolution which brought Russia's Communist government to power. Not all his reforms were successful. He made peasants sell their produce to the state at low fixed prices. They began to grow less and less food. He tried to put right this mistake, but the last seven years have not been easy for rural Russians. Lenin's body will be embalmed and laid in a mausoleum in Red Square. In his honour, Petrograd will be renamed Leningrad.

Josef Stalin (his name means 'man of steel') may be the future leader of the USSR. For the time being he will be one of a council of three people in power, but he is known as an ambitious man.

MUSIC FIT FOR A MONARCH

May 4, London Sir Edward Elgar, the composer, has been made 'Master of the King's Musick'. In this new role, he will be asked to conduct on important state occasions. It is also his duty to compose music for royal events, such as a coronation or royal wedding. Sir Edward conducted one of his best-known works, the first *Pomp and Circumstance* march, at the opening ceremony of the British Empire Exhibition. It includes the tune 'Land of Hope and Glory'.

FINN IS TIRELESS IN OLYMPIC GAMES

July 27, Paris The hero of this year's Olympic Games is Finnish runner Paavo Nurmi. He won six gold medals. He set two Olympic records: he ran the 1500 metres in 3 minutes 53.6 seconds, and the 5000 metres in 14 minutes 31.2 seconds. He had only one hour's rest between the two events. Many other runners have collapsed from heat exhaustion in the present heatwave. Harold Abrahams was the first British competitor to win the 100 metres, equalling the Olympic record. Eric Liddell of Great Britain won the 400 metres.

The Finnish runner Paavo Nurmi streaks away ahead of the competition.

THE BRITISH EMPIRE EXHIBITION OPENS

April 23, Wembley The King opened this huge display today. By pressing a button, he sent a radio message right round the world and back again in 1½ minutes. At the exhibition each Commonwealth country has its own pavilion. The Canadians have a statue of the Prince of Wales made out of butter! The Palaces of Engineering and Industry show the latest in inventions and machinery.

CLIMBERS ARE LOST IN THE HIMALAYAS

June 19, London The third British expedition to climb Mount Everest has ended in tragedy. On June 6 George Mallory and Arthur Irvine started for the summit from a camp high on the mountain. Other climbers last saw them when they were only about 250 metres (800 feet) from the top. Then the mist hid them. They have not returned.

Were Mallory and Irvine the first people ever to reach the summit? We may never know.

LABOUR IS OUT

Nov 6, London The first British Labour government has lasted less than a year. Mr. Stanley Baldwin is back as Conservative Prime Minister. A letter published last month by the British Foreign Office may have turned voters against the Labour Party. It seems to have been written by a leading Russian politician, and urges British workers and Communists to revolt. The Labour Party says the letter is a forgery.

NEWS IN BRIEF . . .

BLACK ACTOR IS THREATENED

May 15, New York Mr. Paul Robeson, the black American singer, has been rehearsing for tonight's opening of *All God's Chillun got Wings*. He plays a black man married to a white woman. The KKK say this is immoral. The star has already received hundreds of threatening letters. One letter said a bomb was going to be planted in the theatre tonight. The police searched the building, but found nothing.

HOSPITAL IN HEART OF AFRICA

April 30, West Africa Dr. Albert Schweitzer returned on Easter Saturday to Lambaréné, 200 km (125 miles) up the River Ogowe in West Africa. By Easter Monday he was seeing patients. He is now rebuilding the hospital he started in 1913 for African villagers. Before he studied medicine, Dr. Schweitzer was a distinguished organist, and principal of a religious college. He is the author of books on Bach, and on Jesus' teaching. His hospital is always crowded.

FOOTBALLER SCORES IN ONE

Oct 11, Huddersfield, England Players taking corner kicks will no longer be allowed to dribble the ball. In future the player may kick the ball once only. This should mean that one man by himself cannot score from a corner kick. But today Billy Smith of Huddersfield Town did just that, and Huddersfield won the League Championships.

FIRST LONG-DISTANCE CALL

June 2, Vancluse, Australia Australia spoke to England last night – by wireless. It is the first time a wireless (rather than telegraph) has been used over such a great distance. The radio pioneer Guglielmo Marconi said that one day there will be telephones all over the world. The calls were made between Poldhu in Cornwall, England, and Vancluse near Sydney, in Australia.

THE ORIENTAL LOOK

Autumn, Paris This year's fashions have a graceful, Japanese feel. Typical of the style are Worth's evening dresses.

1925

April 3   Britain returns to gold standard
July 18   Hitler publishes *Mein Kampf*
July 21   'Monkey' trial in USA ends
Nov 13   Tutankhamun's mummy revealed
Nov 20   Mussolini dictates to Italy

THE AMERICAN DREAM WORLD

AMERICAN BUSINESS BOOMS

Jan 31, New York In America, 'business' has become the most important thing in many people's lives. It is exciting to be able to earn enough for luxuries like cars, washing machines and radios. For entertainment people visit cinemas, night clubs and music halls. Their parents had none of these things.

WHO WOULD WALK IF HE COULD RIDE?

June 30, Detroit Cars have been the talk of this town ever since Mr. Henry Ford set up his factory. His black 'Tin Lizzies' are cheap and reliable. Now the Chrysler Company is trying to persuade rich business people that a six-cylinder *de luxe* car would suit their style better. The car is a symbol of success. Estate agents say that when people buy houses, the garage is as important as the house itself. Everyone wants a big new car.

A PLACE IN THE SUN

Aug 31, Florida There is a housing and land boom in this sunny state. The plots of land are not cheap, but there seem to be plenty of buyers. The houses they build are in all styles: Spanish, Dutch, colonial American. Many of them have swimming pools. This way of life is the setting for a new novel by F. Scott Fitzgerald called *The Great Gatsby*.

PROSPECTS BAD FOR BRITISH TRADE

April 3, London Mr. Winston Churchill, the Chancellor of the Exchequer, is trying to improve the British economy. He has announced a return to the gold standard. This means that the pound has a fixed rate equal to $4.86, as it was in 1913. Mr. John Maynard Keynes, the leading British economist, warns that the true value of the pound has dropped by 10 per cent. British exports cost more and so foreign countries will buy less of them. Already America and Japan are expanding their trade while Britain's trade share grows less. Unless Britain can make quality goods cheaply, and find new markets for them, the future does not look very bright.

IS CHARLES DARWIN RIGHT?

July 21, Tennessee The state of Tennessee has a new law which says that Charles Darwin's theory of evolution may not be taught in schools. The theory says life began with very simple creatures, and all present animals, including humans, evolved over millions of years. Our ancestors, Darwin said, were like apes. Today, Mr. John Scopes has been found guilty of teaching the theory of evolution. The prosecution lawyer, Mr. William Bryan, believes in the Bible creation story of Adam and Eve. Though Mr. Scopes' lawyer, Mr. Clarence Darrow, showed that Mr. Bryan knew nothing about history and modern science, he lost the case. The teacher had clearly broken the law, and he was fined $100. However, Mr. Darrow criticized the new law, saying that ignorant people should not control children's education.

'OUR PRODUCT IS THE BEST'

Oct 30, New York When you have something to sell, it pays to advertise. In America 600,000 people are creating a dream world in which we can all have shining teeth, clear complexions, and 'whiter than white' clothes. Wherever you look you are urged to buy, buy, buy. Even President Coolidge is advertised, with the slogan 'Keep Cool with Coolidge'.

PLAYWRIGHT GIVEN TOP HONOUR

Dec 10, London Mr. George Bernard Shaw has been awarded the Nobel Prize for Literature, after the success of his play, *St. Joan*. It is based on old documents written in France when the French girl, Joan of Arc, was burnt at the stake by the English nearly 500 years ago. Mr. Shaw, who was born in Dublin, began his career as a journalist. His previous plays include *Man and Superman* (1903) and *Pygmalion* (1912).

A scene from the first stage production of *St. Joan* in London. Joan of Arc, dressed as a soldier, rallies her followers against the English enemy, who were trying to conquer France.

IL DUCE DICTATES TO ITALY

Nov 20, Rome Under Signor Mussolini's government malaria has been wiped out in the south; the trains are punctual; and nobody goes on strike. But in spite of these advantages, many Italians are not happy. They do not like being told what to do and what to say. Signor Mussolini has banned all left-wing (Socialist and Communist) parties. Cabinet ministers who do not agree with Fascism have resigned. The newspapers have to print government propaganda.

HITLER PUBLISHES A BOOK

July 18, Germany Herr Hitler wrote *Mein Kampf* (My Struggle) while he was in prison. His book, published today, is a mixture of autobiography, politics, and arguments against the Jews. In the book he also says that people of one nationality should live under one rule. There are hundreds of Germans in Russia, Poland, Czechoslovakia and Austria. Politicians all over Europe are afraid that if he ever came to power, Hitler might try to invade these countries.

NEWS IN BRIEF . . .

THE CHARLESTON HAS ARRIVED

July 30, London Dancers are kicking up their heels, turning in their toes, knocking their knees together and clicking their fingers to the music of the Charleston. In America everybody has already learnt the steps. They say that over there waiters do the Charleston while they carry bowls of soup to their customers!

THE QUEEN IS GIVEN A DOLLS' HOUSE

April 7, Windsor Castle, England Queen Mary has been given a delightful house for a family of dolls only 15 cm (6 inches) tall. It was designed by the famous architect, Sir Edwin Lutyens. Tiny books on the shelves were specially written by some leading authors. Famous painters have supplied the pictures on the walls.

The public has had a chance to see the doll's house this week at the Ideal Homes Exhibition.

THE TRAMP IS BACK

Aug 6, New York Charlie Chaplin's new film is called *The Gold Rush*. It features the famous little tramp with moustache and cane. He is still dressed in a bowler hat too small for him and baggy trousers.

ZIPPERS ARE FASHION NEWS

Autumn, London Large collars and floppy bows are this year's fashion tip. The daring are wearing their skirts above the knee, showing pink flesh-coloured silk or rayon stockings. This is just the thing for dancing the Charleston! The many bangles worn on both arms add to the excitement.

For rainy days you can buy overshoes with automatic fasteners called 'Lightnings' (Americans call them 'zippers'). At the British Empire Exhibition last year visitors zipped and unzipped a sample zipper more than three million times!

THE PHARAOH TUTANKHAMUN WAS ONLY EIGHTEEN

Nov 13, Egypt Dr. Howard Carter has uncovered the mummified body of Tutankhamun. The mummy was covered with gold, and on the Pharaoh's face was a wonderful gold and blue mask. Nearly 150 jewels were scattered over his body. It is not surprising that in ancient times, jewel and treasure thieves broke into royal graves. Here at last is one which they failed to rob. Scientists say that the Pharaoh was only about 18 years old when he died.

The golden mask of Pharaoh Tutankhamun, from about 1340 B.C.

POLICE RAID GANGSTERS' HIDEOUT

Dec 3, New York The police have raided a warehouse where gangsters were storing alcohol. It is the biggest haul since Prohibition began. But people are still hiding 'bootleg' (illegal) whisky or gin in unusual places: hot-water bottles, shoe heels, perfume bottles, Russian boots. Bootleg liquor is not hard to make – it is just raw alcohol with colour and flavouring added. Even if it doesn't taste like the real thing, everyone wants to buy it. Real whisky can still be had on prescription for a variety of ailments – including 'thirstitis'. Doctors have never been so popular!

1926

Jan 9	Saudi Arabia is established
April 21	Princess Elizabeth is born
May 1	Miners strike in Britain
May 5	General strike in Britain
Nov 20	Colour Bar Bill in South Africa

BRITAIN'S GENERAL STRIKE
THOUSANDS ARE OUT ON STRIKE

May 1, London Miners all over England and Wales downed tools today, and picketed the pits. After the 1921 strike, the government paid mine owners so that they could keep wages high. This payment stopped at midnight last night. From today wages have been decreased. In addition, miners will have to work an extra hour each day. The Trades Union Congress (TUC) is asking other unions to join the strike in support of the miners.

TUC CALLS A GENERAL STRIKE

May 10, London For the first time in British history all union members are out on strike. The General Strike started on May 5. The transport workers have stayed at home, but some public transport is still running. University students are driving stranded city commuters to work by bus and train. Electricity and water supplies are still working normally. There were no newspapers until Mr Winston Churchill launched *The British Gazette* this morning. Volunteers are taking copies to the big towns. Food supplies are collected in Hyde Park, and distributed all over the country by soldiers in armoured cars.

Demonstrating strikers clash with police in the street.

THE STRIKE IS AT AN END

May 12, London The TUC has called off the General Strike. The miners are very angry that other union members have let them down. All the other unions – railwaymen, dockers, road transport workers, printers, builders and the rest – have gone back to work. Their own strike will continue. Their motto is: 'Not a penny off the pay, not a minute on the day.'

AFRICA IS THE 'CRADLE OF MANKIND'

Jan, Kimberley, South Africa Mr. Raymond Dart, who studies our very early history, says that Africa is 'the cradle of mankind'. Two years ago, on November 28 1924, he found the skull of a child. He found it at Tuang near Kimberley. Mr Dart thinks the skull belonged to an ape-like creature that lived about 5 million years ago. The skull is more like a human's than an ape's. Mr. Dart says that modern men and women evolved from these creatures. He has given the species the Latin name *Australopithecus*, which means 'Southern Man'. Mr. Dart is only 33 and many of his critics will not take his discoveries seriously.

A NEW KINGDOM IS BORN IN ARABIA

Jan 9, Mecca, Arabia Abd al-Aziz ibn Sa'ud is one of the most powerful Arab leaders of this century. He left Kuwait, where his family had been exiled, 25 years ago. Now he has become ruler of most of Arabia. Yesterday in the holy city of Mecca he was crowned King of Najd and the Hejaz. He has called his kingdom Saudi Arabia, after the Sa'ud name.

POVERTY FORCES MINERS BACK TO WORK

Nov 19, northern England and Wales After seven months without pay, the miners cannot hold out in their strike any longer. They have gone back to work. Their families have suffered badly, and are living on bread and margarine, tea and skimmed milk. The men will now have to work for longer hours, and for lower wages.

AFRICANS BARRED FROM WELL-PAID JOBS

Nov 20, Pretoria, South Africa South Africa, along with Canada, New Zealand and Australia, has become a self-governing dominion. This will make no difference to the majority of South Africans – the black people. By the 'Colour Bar' Bill, they may no longer compete with whites and coloureds (people of mixed race) for highly-paid jobs. In future they will be employed mainly in the mines and factories as unskilled labourers. Women will only find work as domestic servants or nursery maids. Africans cannot vote, so they have no legal way of changing this situation.

A ROYAL BABY IS BORN

April 21, London The Duchess of York has given birth to her first child, a daughter. She will be called Elizabeth Alexandra Mary. She is third in line to the throne, after her uncle and her father, so there is a chance that she may one day be Queen.

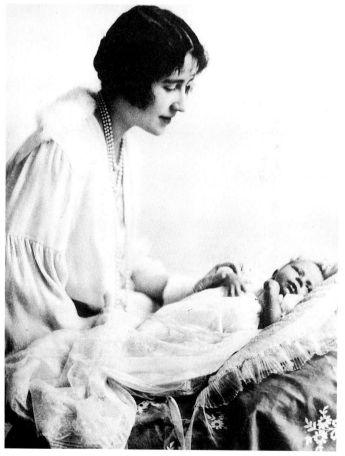

The Duchess of York with Princess Elizabeth

NEWS IN BRIEF . . .

INVENTOR DEMONSTRATES MOVING PICTURES

Jan 26, London Radio waves have been successfully used to transmit pictures as well as sound. The Scottish inventor, Mr. John Logie Baird, showed a moving picture on a small screen today. He did this without a film projector. He is continuing to experiment with his invention. If it is successful, in the future it may be possible to see moving pictures transmitted into our own homes.

Mr. Baird and his TV apparatus

WILL ROCKETS FLY THROUGH SPACE?

March 16, Washington A rocket enthusiast, Dr. Robert Goddard, has built his own rockets and launched them from the back of a truck for some time. They were about a metre high, and farmers complained that they landed in their fields! He has now sent one high into the atmosphere from a metal platform. Other scientists point out that, as far as we know, there is no air in space. A rocket would not be able to fly to the moon through a vacuum. Only time will tell if Dr. Goddard proves them wrong.

PAINTER LEAVES IMPRESSIONS BEHIND

Dec 5, Giverny, France The French painter Claude Monet died today. He was 86. Monet was an 'impressionist' painter, fascinated by the different colours produced by light and shadow. He made a superb water garden at his home. He painted the waterlilies there literally hundreds of times.

HOW'S THAT?

Sept 15, London Jack Hobbs, Surrey's champion cricketer, has beaten his own record. In the recent match against Middlesex he scored 316 not out.

HYSTERICS AFTER STAR'S DEATH

Aug 25, USA Rudolph Valentino, the star of romantic movies such as *The Sheikh* (1921), died last week of appendicitis. He was only 31. The handsome actor drew crowds to his films and had thousands of fans. Many young ladies are in mourning, and one young dancer has even poisoned herself. Thirty thousand people went to his funeral.

MACHINES REPLACE FARM ANIMALS

Oct 31, Sussex, England Six oxen have been taken out of their plough harness for the last time on a Sussex farm. The plough team was the last in England.

HOUDINI WAS UNPREPARED FOR SHOCK

Oct 31, Detroit, USA The entertainer Harry Houdini is dead. He told a group of students that his stomach muscles could take the strongest punches. One of them hit him hard when he was unprepared, and burst his appendix. Houdini drew huge audiences by his 'magic' escapes from trunks locked and tied with ropes. Often he would be chained, too. His latest trick was to stay under water for 91 minutes with air that would last only about 6 minutes. Nobody knew how he did it.

Get out of that! Harry Houdini the escapologist in his heyday.

1927

CHINA

CHIANG KAI-SHEK OPPOSES CHINA'S WARLORDS

Jan 31, Shanghai General Chiang Kai-shek, leader of the Chinese Nationalists, is winning China's long civil war. Soldiers of his enemies, the powerful 'warlords' of the north, are deserting in thousands. They are joining the Nationalist army, which is now near Shanghai.

THE NATIONALISTS CAPTURE SHANGHAI

April 21, Shanghai General Chiang Kai-shek's army has entered Shanghai, China's richest port. Factory workers and dockers in the city, led by Communist trade union officials, had already overcome all opposition. The Nationalists hardly had to fire a single shot to gain control of the city.

Chiang Kai-shek greeted at Hankow

THE NATIONALISTS TURN ON THE COMMUNISTS

April 30, Shanghai Chiang Kai-shek and his leaders have turned against the Communists. Nationalist troops have been hunting them down and brutally killing them. Thousands of workers in Shanghai, who only last week helped the Nationalists gain the city, have been massacred.

THE COMMUNISTS ARE IN HIDING

Dec 31, China A leader in the Communist Party, Mao Tse-tung, is in hiding in the hills of central China. He has been involved in several failed uprisings. There are less than 10,000 Communists left in China, but they refuse to give in.

A GENERAL STRIKE MAY NEVER HAPPEN AGAIN

June 23, London Today parliament passed the Trades Disputes Act. It is now illegal for workers to go on strike in support of strikers in a different industry, as happened last year.

WHY THE COPS CAN'T CATCH THE ROBBERS

July, Chicago Besides selling alcohol illegally, Chicago's gangsters are forcing money from small businesses by 'protection'. Each week they demand money from unfortunate shopkeepers or garage owners. If they refuse, their business premises may be mysteriously destroyed. Police cannot arrest top gangster Al Capone because he has a powerful friend – the mayor of Chicago.

FAME FOR PILOT OF THE *SPIRIT OF ST. LOUIS*

June 13, New York Mr. Charles Lindbergh drove through the streets of New York today like a conquering hero. His name is known to everyone because of his non-stop flight across the Atlantic last month. His one-engined plane, the *Spirit of St. Louis*, contained neither radio, parachute nor map. During the whole 33½-hour journey he had to rely on his eyes and his sense of direction. When he landed in Paris he had travelled 5800 km (3600 miles).

As his motorcade drove through New York today, office workers made paper streamers from old files and phone books and showered them down from their skyscraper windows. Mr. Lindbergh has received 3½ million fan letters!

Mr. Charles Lindbergh, the solo pilot

The start of the historic flight as *The Spirit of St. Louis* takes off from Long Island.

NEWS IN BRIEF . . .

LAST NIGHT AT THE PROMS

Aug 14, London The BBC broadcast the Promenade Concert at the Queen's Hall for the first time last night. The programme, conducted by Sir Henry Wood, began with Elgar's 'Cockaigne' Overture, a work which Elgar called 'a picture of London'.

BABE RUTH IS A WINNER

Sept 30, New York Baseball champion 'Babe' Ruth has scored a record of 60 home runs in the league season, which started in April. Ruth is the best left-handed pitcher in the American League. The New York Yankees bought him from the Boston Red Sox in 1913. Since then the Yankees have never looked back.

Babe Ruth dressed for action

THE TALKIES ARE HERE

Oct 6, Hollywood The release of Al Jolson's new film, *The Jazz Singer,* is a special event. The songs he sings come from a special sound track attached to the moving pictures. But the most amazing thing is that, for the first time, you can actually hear his voice speaking. "You ain't heard nothing yet," he drawls.

Cinemas will soon be showing other talkies. Greta Garbo and Conrad Veidt are two 'silent' stars who are hastily learning English.

WARNER BROS. SUPREME TRIUMPH
AL JOLSON
IN
'The **JAZZ SINGER**'

TOP DESIGNER FASHIONS

Spring, London Dress designers are full of ideas this year. Worth has put the waist back above the hips. His hemline comes just below the knee, though his evening wear reaches the calf. A new designer, Elsa Schiaparelli, introduces more casual wear for daytime. Her short pleated skirts and lightweight sweaters are bought by fashion-conscious ladies who also want comfort. Norman Hartnell favours longer skirts for his models.

YEHUDI MENUHIN, A YOUNG MUSICIAN TO WATCH

Feb 13, Paris An 11-year-old American violinist, Yehudi Menuhin, is delighting audiences here. At his first European concert he played Tchaikovsky's Violin Concerto. This little blond boy asked the leader of the orchestra to tune his violin for him. And when a string broke half-way through, he waited calmly while the leader fitted a new one. Yehudi Menuhin started to learn the violin when he was four. Two years later he played at a Young People's Concert in San Francisco. Critics say he is a remarkable player and has a great future ahead of him.

GOODBYE TO THE TIN LIZZIES

Dec 1, New York, USA Mr. Henry Ford is going to stop making Model T cars. Over the last 20 years about 15 million 'Tin Lizzies' have been sold. Ford's slogan was, 'You can have any colour you like, as long as it's black.' General Motors are now producing cars in a range of colours. Their cars have six cylinders and modern hydraulic brakes. From today, Ford's Model T will be replaced by the Model A, with a self-starter, shock absorbers and an unbreakable windscreen.

1928

HARD TIMES IN RUSSIA

TROTSKY IS IN DISGRACE

Jan 16, Moscow A few years ago, Leon Trotsky was a hero. He was one of the leaders of the Russian revolution. But Stalin forced Trotsky to give up control of the Red Army and dismissed him from the Communist Party. Now Trotsky has been moved to a prison in the loneliest part of the country. Trotsky is one of 30 Soviet leaders arrested on Stalin's orders.

WORKERS ARE BLAMED FOR POOR ECONOMY

Oct 1, Moscow Stalin wants to make the USSR an advanced technical country. The new Dnieper Dam will supply electricity. The power plant at the dam will be the largest in the world.

Stalin has a large force of secret police. They told him that coal miners were holding back production. Of the 52 miners brought to trial, five have been executed. Nobody knows whether they were really guilty, or forced to make a confession.

STALIN MUST BE OBEYED

Sept 30, Moscow Many Bolshevik leaders are alarmed at the way Stalin is running the country, but they dare not say so. Only one critic has spoken out. Nikolai Bukharin has published an article in *Pravda* defending the peasants and farmers. Stalin is not likely to allow him to go unpunished.

CHIANG KAI-SHEK HEADS NORTH

CHINESE AND JAPANESE CLASH

May 11, Shantung province Chinese Nationalist troops under General Chiang Kai-shek have marched north and entered Tsinan, a town where 2000 Japanese civilians are living. When 11 of these civilians were killed by Nationalist soldiers, the Japanese government sent troops to protect its people. The Japanese general demanded that Chinese officers should be publicly punished for the killings. Chiang Kai-shek refused, and so the Japanese attacked and killed over a thousand Chinese soldiers. The rest were forced out of the city. They joined other sections of Chiang's army, which is marching towards Peking.

Josef Stalin, the new strong man in Russia

NATIONALISTS REACH THEIR GOAL

June 4, Peking The Nationalists captured Peking today, after its governor was killed as he fled to Manchuria. Peking has been the capital city, and the home of China's emperors, for 900 years. There is no longer an emperor, but it was necessary for the Nationalists to capture such an important town. However, the new capital is to be at Nanking, in central China. Chiang Kai-shek will be China's first president.

IS THE NEW IMMIGRANT A PRINCESS?

Feb 6, New York Ever since Tsar Nicholas II of Russia and his family were murdered in 1918 by the Bolsheviks, there have been rumours about their deaths. Americans are now wondering if one of the royal children survived the massacre. A young woman arrived in New York today. She claims that she is the Tsar's youngest daughter, Princess Anastasia. Many people are doubtful. It seems unlikely that the Bolsheviks would have allowed a member of the royal family to escape.

PRINCE RUSHES TO THE KING'S BEDSIDE

Dec 2, London The Prince of Wales arrived home today after returning at great speed from East Africa. He had been sent for because of the King's grave illness. The Prince took a ship from Tanganyika to Italy. Then Mussolini arranged for him to travel in his private train across Europe. The King's health is improving after an operation. (*Tanganyika is now Tanzania.*)

ANOTHER 'FIRST' FOR WOMEN AT THE OLYMPICS

Aug 12, Amsterdam Women competed for the first time in track events at this year's games in the Netherlands. Germany also took part, for the first time since the war, and sent 300 athletes to the games.

Paavo Nurmi of Finland, who did so well in 1924, added one more gold and two silver medals to his collection. Hockey is back in the games, and India was the winner. Its team scored 29 goals altogether, and none of its opponents scored at all.

The victorious Indian hockey team in action

WOMEN MAY GO TO THE POLLS

June 18, London Today the Equal Franchise Bill was passed. For the first time, British women over the age of 21 may vote in elections. This will add five million people to the voters' roll. By calling this the 'flapper' vote, some people seem to imply that women will not vote responsibly.

By a coincidence, Mrs. Emmeline Pankhurst died this week. Mrs Pankhurst led the campaign for women's right to vote, so her life's ambition has been fulfilled.

Lunchtime voters leave a polling station.

WATER, WATER EVERYWHERE

January 7, London After last year's white Christmas and freezing blizzards at New Year, there has been a sudden thaw. Melting snow and high tides have led to a great flood all over London. Fourteen people have drowned. The *Daily News* reports: "In some places the water was half way up the walls of ground floor rooms". It is the worst flood here for hundreds of years.

POLAR EXPLORER KILLED

June 20, Spitzbergen, Norway The Norwegian explorer, Roald Amundsen, died today when his seaplane crashed into the Arctic Ocean. He was trying to rescue a fellow explorer, who has been stranded on the ice for a month after his airship was forced to land. Two years ago the two friends were the first people to fly over the North Pole. In 1911, Amundsen achieved his highest goal: his expedition was the first to reach the South Pole on foot – 30 days ahead of the British explorer, Captain Scott.

NEWS IN BRIEF . . .

LOUIS IS KING OF THE JAZZ AGE

July 20, Chicago Jazz has conquered America, and nowhere is it better played than in Chicago. Here Louis Armstrong ('Satchmo') plays trombone or cornet, and sings to his band's music. Armstrong's Hot Five play brilliant solo passages. They are also famous for their 'scat' singing, meaningless 'de-doo-be-doo' words, and for slowing up or quickening the beat. Their latest record, just released, is 'West End Blues'. Jazz is especially popular with young people.

LAND SPEED RECORD

Feb 19, Florida Malcolm Campbell, the British racing driver, has beaten the land speed record in the specially-built car *Bluebird*. Over two laps, on the racing track at Daytona, his car averaged a speed of 214.8 mph.

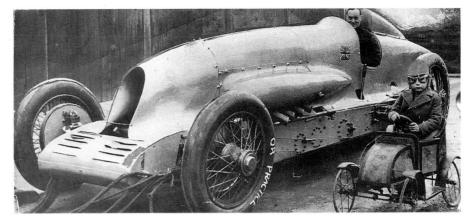

Malcolm Campbell in *Bluebird*. His son Donald is in the pedal car.

ETNA ERUPTS

Nov 12, Sicily Molten lava is pouring down the slopes of the volcano Mt. Etna towards the town of Catania, between the mountain and the sea. Mt. Etna erupted a week ago, and since then the lava has overwhelmed villages and crops on the mountain slopes. The townspeople of Catania are afraid that if it continues, their homes will be in danger. People living in this region are used to small eruptions, but this is one of the largest ever recorded. The erupting volcano glows red at night, and is an amazing sight.

For sale
Semi-detached house in London suburbs. Drawing room, dining room, kitchen, hall. Three bedrooms, bathroom. Price: £550.

MICKEY MOUSE, FILM STAR, SPEAKS

Nov 18, Hollywood Walt Disney's cartoon character, Mickey Mouse, first starred in *Plane Crazy* earlier this year. That was a silent film. Today you can see – and hear – Mickey in the talkie *Steamboat Willie*.

FLYING DOCTORS

May, Sydney, Australia To cover the vast territory of the 'outback', an Australian doctor came up with a new idea: he bought a plane and engaged a pilot to take him to his patients. Other doctors have followed his example and together they have formed the Flying Doctor Service.

ENTER POOH AND PIGLET AGAIN

Oct 11, London Mr. A. A. Milne has published a second children's book, *The House at Pooh Corner*. It continues the story of Christopher Robin, Pooh, and all the other animals we have met already in *Winnie-the-Pooh*. Mr. Milne has also written two books of poetry for children.

1929

FALL OF THE MIGHTY DOLLAR
SHARE PRICES ARE RISING RAPIDLY

Sept 3, New York   Fewer houses have been built this year, and fewer cars sold. The American economy may be slowing down. In spite of this, the new President, Mr. Herbert Hoover, hailed this year as one of 'happiness and hopefulness'. For many Americans, happiness means wealth, and the creation of even more wealth by buying stocks and shares. Today Wall Street, the American Stock Exchange, sold a record number of shares. The price of all shares is still rising. Those who have sold shares recently have made their fortunes.

'Black Tuesday' as Stock Market Falls

Oct 24, New York   Last Thursday share prices began to fall dramatically. People panicked and tried to sell their shares. Brokers (dealers) were unable to cope with all the customers. As thousands of shares were sold, the price fell even further. More and more people tried to get their money back. The result of this was that even more shares were sold – and so the decline went on.

When the stock market opened this morning, traffic came to a standstill as thousands of investors blocked the road. They were trying to push their way into the Stock Exchange, to sell shares that had become almost worthless. After 16 million shares had been sold, prices dropped to rock-bottom. There is an air of disbelief in America tonight. Many investors face ruin.

A ruined investor makes a desperate attempt to raise money after the Wall Street crash.

AFTER THE CRASH

Dec 31, New York With businesses becoming bankrupt every day, the number of unemployed has risen to over three million. There are no bank loans available because the banks are also in great difficulties. Some people have committed suicide rather than face the loss of all their property, and huge debts which they could not pay. This is an unhappy end to the decade. Americans are slowly realizing that the boom years of prosperity are over.

THE SMALLEST STATE IN THE WORLD

Feb 11, Rome Today the Pope and Signor Mussolini have ended a long disagreement between the Church and the Italian government. In future the pope's Palace, the church of St. Peter, and all the great buildings nearby, will form a separate state. It will be called Vatican City. The pope will be its ruler, and the Italian government will have no control over its affairs. Signor Mussolini promises that all schools in Italy will teach the Catholic faith.

GANGSTERS KILLED ON ST. VALENTINE'S DAY

Feb 14, Chicago The war between rival gangs came to a climax today. Al Capone's gang, dressed as policemen, raided a garage where a rival gang was waiting for a delivery of illegal alcohol. They lined the men up against a wall then opened fire with machine guns and killed them all. But the leader of the gang, Bugsy Moran, was not in the garage. Though Bugsy has lost half his men, his sideline is flourishing: he supplies expensive wreaths for gangsters' funerals!

THE FIGHT AGAINST DISEASE

Feb 14, London A leading scientist, Professor Alexander Fleming, spoke about his research to the Medical Research Club yesterday. Last year he noticed that a mould was growing on some bacteria in his laboratory, and killing them. He began to study the mould, and has made from it a substance called penicillin. He is going to test this further.

FARMERS ARE BADLY OFF

Sept 30, England The drought this summer followed a severe winter. The farmers found it difficult to feed their animals. Many farmers bought their land with bank loans when market prices were high. Some have lost their farms because they could no longer afford the interest on their loans. To save the cost of labour, pigs are being fattened in sheds instead of running free in fields. Hens are also being kept indoors in 'batteries'. Out-of-work agricultural workers are turning to the towns for new jobs.

MUSTAFA KEMAL REFORMS TURKEY

Dec 31, Constantinople In only six years, Mustafa Kemal has made Turkey into an efficient modern state. The Turkish language is now written in Roman and not Arabic script. Education and the legal system are no longer controlled by Islamic teachers and lawyers. No man may have more than one wife. And the red fez, which every man in Turkey wore, is no longer worn – by law.

Arabic and new Roman shop signs in Constantinople

NEWS IN BRIEF . . .

LIVING APART BY LAW

May, Pretoria, South Africa The South African government has decided to have separate schools and housing areas for Africans and Europeans. They argue that the two races have different cultures. Africans see this as an attempt to keep them less well educated and in inferior jobs.

THE TREASURE SEEKERS

June 27, Italy Gold and silver valued at more than a million pounds was lost when the P & O liner *Egypt* sank in the Atlantic in 1922. Many salvage crews have tried to recover the treasure, but none has succeeded because the wreck is 130 metres (142 yards) deep. Today Signor Aristide Franceschi has become the first diver ever to reach this depth. He stayed under water for nearly two hours. In spite of this record-breaking effort, Franceschi did not see any sign of the wreck.

Gabrielle 'Coco' Chanel

GERMAN AND BRITISH AIRSHIPS' HISTORIC FLIGHTS

Oct 14, London The largest airship ever built, the *R101*, made its first flight today. It can carry about 50 passengers. This is Britain's answer to the German *Graf Zeppelin*, which recently completed its round-the-world flight, taking 21½ days. It stopped only three times on this enormous journey. Zeppelins were designed by the German Count Ferdinand Zeppelin.

The *R101* airship by London's Tower Bridge

DRESS SENSE

Spring, Paris To go with the new short hairstyle called the Eton crop, French designer Coco Chanel has introduced a collection of smart, practical clothes in wool jersey. She uses plain pastel colours or stripes to equal effect. She dresses up the simple lines with costume jewellery and rows of beads. Chanel says, "I make fashions that women can breathe in, feel comfortable in and look good in." Another designer, Elsa Schiaparelli, is so successful that she now employs about 2000 people in her 26 workrooms.

EVIDENCE OF THE FLOOD

Nov, London Sir Leonard Woolley, a British archaeologist, has excavated the ruins of Ur, an ancient town on the River Euphrates, south of Baghdad. Ur flourished in about 2000 B.C. Below its ruins Sir Leonard came to a layer of mud 2½ metres thick. Under this layer of mud were ruins of an even earlier town. Sir Leonard believes that the mud layer was deposited by a great flood, probably the one we call Noah's Flood, as described in the Bible. The mud layer has been dated to about 4000 B.C.

PEOPLE OF THE TWENTIES

Sir John Berry Hobbs, cricketer 1882–1963

Jack Hobbs started playing cricket for Surrey when he was 23, and he played for England from 1907 to 1930. In his long career in first-class cricket he made 197 centuries. He scored over 6000 runs altogether. His fielding was brilliant, and so was his bowling: during the 1920s and 1930s he ran out more batsmen than did any other bowler. He continued playing cricket long after most players would have retired. As a man he was modest, gentle and kind. He was perhaps the greatest cricketer of all time. Other players called him 'The Master'.

Marie Stopes 1880–1958

Marie Stopes was born in Edinburgh, and took her degree in botany and geology in London. Her primary career was as a specialist in fossil plants. But after a failed first marriage, she wrote *Married Love* in 1918, and later *Wise Parenthood*. These were the first books dealing frankly with sex in marriage, and with birth control. Marie Stopes opened a Mothers' Clinic for Birth Control in London, and later published the first book on contraception. Her work drew fierce attacks from the Church and the medical profession. Dr. Stopes did more than any other single person to control the population explosion in Europe in the 1900s.

Charlie Chaplin, actor and director, 1889–1977

As a boy in London, Chaplin learnt his comedy acting in the music halls. He was invited to Hollywood in 1913 by the Keystone film studio. Here he invented the character of the sad little tramp. In the 1920s he was directing great comedies such as *The Kid* and *The Gold Rush*. When talking pictures arrived, Chaplin ignored them: *City Lights* (1931) and *Modern Times* (1936) were both silent comedies. During World War II he directed and starred in *The Great Dictator*, which made fun of Hitler and the Nazis.

(James) Ramsay MacDonald 1866–1937

Born in Scotland, MacDonald began his career as a journalist and was secretary of the Labour Party in 1906. Elected to parliament in 1906, he led the parliamentary Labour Party from 1911. He became the first Labour prime minister in 1924, and made some reforms in housing and education. His main interests were in foreign affairs, and he had a strong voice in the League of Nations. In 1931 he led an all-party government, but resigned because of ill-health in 1935.

Mustafa Kemal, Turkish leader 1881–1938

Kemal was born to poor parents but was very successful in his army career and rose to head a government in Ankara at the time when the British occupied Constantinople after World War I. He deposed the Sultan and reformed the government. He made sweeping changes in Turkey's legal system and schools. He completely changed the country's outlook, to bring it into line with modern European society. After his rule, Turkish men no longer wore pantaloons (wide trousers) and a fez. Mustafa Kemal became known as Kemal Atatürk, the 'Chief Turk'.

Al Jolson, entertainer 1886-1950

Al Jolson was born Asa Yoelson, in Lithuania, but his parents emigrated to America when he was a child. When he was nine his parents changed his name to Al Jolson. He became a street entertainer with his brother Harry a year later and at 12 joined a circus. In 1909 he joined a troupe of minstrel singers, who blackened their faces and sang spirituals and minstrel songs. He sang, someone said, "with a peculiar buzzing note". In 1918 the Gershwin song 'Swannee' became his signature tune. Famous songs of the twenties include 'If you knew Susie' and 'Sonny Boy'. He made three silent films before starring in *The Jazz Singer* in 1927. After 'talkies' arrived he starred in several films and in 1946 he dubbed the songs for his own life history, *The Jolson Story*, in which he was played by Larry Parks.

Greta Garbo, film star b. 1905

Greta Garbo was born in Sweden. She won a scholarship to drama school, and was picked out by a leading film director as a future star. He took her to Hollywood, where her acting ability brought her into the limelight. Greta Garbo was a very private person, and she avoided publicity. Her fame rests on only a few films, from the early days of Hollywood. When talking pictures were introduced she learnt English, but she never lost her Swedish accent. At the age of 36 she left Hollywood, and never made another film.

Albert Einstein, physicist 1879–1955

Einstein, born in Germany, was a genius who made many scientific discoveries that have changed the way in which scientists work.

By the age of 36 one of his discoveries had won him the Nobel Prize for Physics (1921). This discovery has to do with the effect of coloured light on electrons. His Theory of Relativity states that 'all motion is relative'. It says that matter can be turned into energy. This is the principle behind the atomic bomb.

When Hitler came to power, Einstein, who was Jewish, became an American citizen. Up to his death he was working on ways to control the energy of the atom.

For the first time ever

1920	USA	Kellogg's All Bran is marketed
		Chanel No. 5 perfume
	UK	Catgut is used as surgical thread
		Roads are given letters and numbers
		Scholarships for University places
1921	Canada	Insulin is used for diabetic patients
	USA	A lie detector is invented
		Vitamins D and E are discovered
		Cars must have tax discs and log books
1922	Japan	An aircraft carrier is launched
	USA	Telephone exchanges are mechanized
		Tinned baby food on sale
	Switzerland	Winter sports include a slalom race
	UK	The first radio broadcasts are made
		Pilots need a licence to fly
	Germany	A Count Dracula film is shown
1923	UK	Hearing aids are available
	Denmark	Whooping cough vaccine
	Spain	An autogiro, the first kind of helicopter, flies
	USA	Iced lollies are on sale
		Paper tissues are made by Kleenex
	Switzerland	A self-winding watch is invented
	Germany	A planetarium opens
1924	Sweden	Aga stoves are sold
	USA	An electroencephalogram (EEG) registers brain waves
	Italy	A motorway is opened
1925	France	Films shown in Cinemascope
	USA	An electric gramophone is marketed
	UK	Insulin in use
		Cars have dipped headlights
1926	UK	There are dodgem cars at the fair
		Pedestrian crossings are necessary because of increase in traffic
	Norway	Aerosol cans are invented
	New Zealand	Family allowances
	France	Aqualung invented

1927	USA	An iron lung is used for polio patients
	UK	Heinz bottles a salad cream
		Electric blanket on the market
		Kirbigrips are on sale
1928	USA	Sticky tape is on sale
	UK	Automatic record changers
		Fleming discovers penicillin
	Germany	Geiger counter invented
	Italy	Speak-your-weight machines
1929	UK	The Pony Club is founded
		Some milk is delivered in cartons
	USA	The latest toy is the Yo-Yo
		A quartz clock is invented

New words and expressions

New inventions, habits and occupations bring new words into the language. People also invent new slang. These are some of the words and phrases used for the first time in the 1920s in England and America.

addict
on the air
beautician
blind date
the blues
breakthrough
broadcast programmes
Cellophane
check-up
columnist
corgi
crash helmet
executive
Fascist
Fleet Air Arm
gatecrasher
gimmick
he's cuckoo
header (football)
hitch-hiker
hoover

insulin
Interpol
jazz
jive
knitwear
lead someone up the
   garden path
left-wing
motorcade
nitwit
on the air
one over the eight
penicillin
plastic
permanent wave (perm)
potato crisps
to be pretty dim
radio
shingled hair
telephone kiosk
you're my cup of tea
tip-off

How many of these words and expressions are still used today? Do you know what they all mean?

Glossary

black market: the sale of goods illegally at high prices, when they are in short supply.

Bolsheviks: Russian political party. The original Communist party.

diabetic: a person whose body does not absorb sugar properly. A hormone called insulin is used to control this condition.

on the dole: receiving social security money.

dub: to add a sound track onto a film.

embalm: to preserve after death with special ointments.

erupt: to blow up (volcano), throwing out rocks and lava.

Fascists: Italian political party, anti-Communist.

flapper: a young woman in the 1920s, usually thought to be rather scatterbrained.

franchise: the right to vote.

general strike: strike in which workers in many industries join to support the original strikers.

lava: a red-hot liquid. When it cools, it becomes a hard black rock.

mandate: a country given in trust to one of the winning nations after the Great War.

mausoleum: a large tomb.

motorcade: a line of motor cars in a procession.

picket: people who stand outside a workplace to persuade others to join a strike.

Prohibition: the banning of alcohol during the 1920s in the United States.

propaganda: information designed to change people's point of view.

protectorate: an underdeveloped country in the care of a stronger one.

reparations: compensation for war damage.

Further Reading

The Twenties: R J Unstead. Macdonald, 1973

A History of the 20th Century: D. B. O'Callaghan. Longman 1987

The Twenties in Vogue: Carolyn Hall. Octopus 1983

Picture History of the 20th Century series; *The 1920s*: Richard Tames. Franklin Watts 1991

20s and 30s Style: Horsham. Apple 1989

How we used to live 1902 – 1926: Freda Kelsall. A & C Black 1985

The Twentieth Century: R J Unstead. A & C Black 1974

Costume in Context: The 1920s & 1930s: Jennifer Ruby. Batsford, 1988

Fashions of a Decade: 1920s: Jacqueline Herald. Batsford, 1991

Finding out about life in Britain in 1920s: Monica Hodgson. Batsford, 1987

Growing up in the 1920s: Amanda Clarke. Batsford, 1981

Portrait of a Decade series; *The 1920s*: Betty Williams. Batsford, 1989

Living through History series; *Roaring Twenties*: Graham Mitchell. Batsford 1986